DEALING WITH BREAKUP

GUIDE ON HOW TO RECOVER FROM BREAKUP

VICTOR AJAYI

TABLE OF CONTENT

INTRODUCTION

You could or might not be aware of what went wrong that caused you and your ex to break up. In order to ensure that it does not occur again, you would think about avoiding the same mistakes. You would most likely hope that when you are ready to start a new relationship, it will work out.

Learn everything you require right here in this eBook.

CHAPTER 1
BE SURE

Never assume you understand what you or your partner needs. Don't think you know what will happen next

You believe you are familiar with your partner. You erroneously believe you are aware of what to do next and your partner's response. What if you don't really comprehend it well, which leads to all the confusion that follows?

Love your partner as yourself. Always take good care of your partner. Take part in your partner's activities, events, etc. Keep in touch with your partner. Make a call or text your partner while you're at work. You should occasionally give your lover surprises as well to make them laugh.

Stay upbeat. Avoid negative feelings if you want to be in a healthy relationship. Avoid allowing yourself to feel bad or to imagine the worst possible outcome for the circumstance you both, are currently in. To combat the stress brought on by your daily activities, try to maintain your composure.

Keep your heart open. You would probably feel wounded after a breakup, and no matter how hard you try to bury it, it still lingers in your heart. Don't bring up the old relationship when starting a new one. Do not let your past relationship affect your current relationship. Don't worry about falling in love again either. You can tell whether you are continuing in the right or bad relationship by keeping an open heart.

CHAPTER 2
SHARE THE SAME GOAL

A fantastic strategy to keep the proper connection going is to have a shared goal for the relationship or in life. Knowing the shared goal between yourselves will make it easier to determine whether or not this is the proper relationship. So, before starting a relationship, one should think about what they both have in common.

You are aware of where your relationship will go. You will know your directions in the relationship or in life if you share a mission. It is preferable that both parties are prepared for marriage rather than just one.

You are able to converse clearly with one another. You are aware of your partner's needs, requests, and perhaps even their thought processes. You'll be able to participate in your partner's daily activities if you have a shared goal. As a result, there are less misunderstandings.

It is simpler to communicate feelings to one another. You will have a clear understanding of his or her circumstances and what they are at this time. Consequently, he or she will believe in you and express themselves more. Because you are kind and understanding, he or she will feel comfortable speaking to you about their feelings and views. When you are confident that he or she comprehends your circumstances, you will also feel better and be less guarded when you express your feelings or emotions to them. Together, you can search for solutions. It will be challenging to make things right if either spouse has different perspectives on the relationship or anything they are dealing with. You will be able to respond to and resolve problems with a shared purpose. Additionally, because you both share a similar way of thinking, you will be able to respect your partner's approach to problem-solving.

CHAPTER 3
MAINTAINING A LONG-TERM RELATIONSHIP

You would want to be in a nice relationship that is better than your previous one whether you are a high school student or an adult looking for fresh love and a new life. You must realize that not all relationships are meant to last forever, others are only meant to last for a short period of time. Make sure you are aware of how to keep a long-term relationship going.

Your relatives and friends are also involved in your relationship, in addition to yourself and your partner. As a result, you must understand and know how to treat your partner's family and friends carefully in order to preserve a good relationship with them. If you and your partner are having problems, this will help to avoid conflicts.

Let go and move on. The ultimate act of love is to forgive. Make an effort to forget all the wrongdoings that your partner committed. Try to put terrible things from the past or the day before in the past and focus on a better today and tomorrow. Don't also hold your partner responsible for everything. Give each other support. Everybody requires help from their partner, especially when maintaining a relationship, whether it be in the form of material assistance, emotional support, or spiritual guidance. To avoid having a relationship that is merely temporary, it is imperative to earn and provide your partner's trust. Always pay attention to him or her and consider what your partner needs.

Find a straightforward solution. Find a quick solution to problems and settle disagreements with your companion. Before retiring to bed, it is essential to resolve the day's issues. Say your thoughts. If at all feasible, talk about the situation and invite your partner to join you in resolving the issues. Be mature in how you handle the situation and make logical decisions before acting.

CHAPTER 4
FOLLOW YOUR INSTINCTS

The most truths about you and your spouse may always be found by listening to your gut or following your instincts. Being truthful with oneself means paying attention to your gut. Particularly when something seems to be awry, your instincts will guide you toward the best course of action for handling the situation. Overanalyzing might occasionally cause you to appear uncertain in your remarks or behaviors, which breeds mistrust, suspicion, and misunderstanding.

Do not suppress your emotions. It's possible that we prefer a certain approach to issue solving because it feels right. You suspect that your partner is cheating on you since you find it weird that he or she arrives home late every night. It takes gut instinct to ask if you truly want to know the answers to such a question and to believe the answers. If you continue to try to conceal the issue, you can start to question your partner and have disagreements. So, trust your instincts to steer clear of any mistakes. Avoid thinking too much. When something seems off, try not to overthink or analyze it. Overanalyzing could divert your focus from the happy emotions and increase the negative ones. This could put you through needless stress, which would harm your relationship.

Speak out. When anything has you worried, speak out and express your concerns. The doubts building up are lessened by speaking up. Talk to your partner about the situation. Describe your thoughts or the causes behind your actions. Make an effort to comprehend and properly express your feelings. It's crucial to follow your instincts, but you also need to know how to communicate so as not to upset your partner. Do not overthink, and evaluate whether your response may or may not hurt your relationship, and most importantly, your partner's feelings.

CHAPTER 5
STOP BEING POSESSIVE

Being possessive is typically brought on by feelings of fear or distrust toward your partner; it may also result from previous failed relationships. Being overly possessive about your partner will make them feel burdened, which will damage your relationship. Respect your personal limits and those of your Partner at all times.

Leave your lover alone. Be considerate of your partner's privacy. Understanding your partner's everyday activities, work life, etc. is important, but not in minute detail. Avert making excessive demands and interfering with your partner's personal decisions. Plan your time together so that you can avoid pressuring your partner to connect with you too frequently.

Provide options to your partner. Give him/her the option to decide what to do each day. Don't make decisions for everyone; recognize that your partner may also have different choices. In addition, give him or her an opportunity to pursue interests and hobbies. This would convey to your lover that you genuinely care about them. Treat yourself. Give yourself some alone time. Visit your family and friends, go shopping, or mingle with people by playing sports; you can also occasionally give yourself some credit for your accomplishments. By taking care of yourself, you can keep yourself from becoming overly dependent on your partner, which could make you more self-assured and less possessive of them.

Make an effort to develop your unique individuality. It's time to pay attention to your true wants and interests, which you might have forgotten about because you share a home with your partner. Engage in your passions and regain your self-confidence.

CHAPTER 6
YOU COME OUT BETTER AFTER A BREAKUP

You become stronger after a breakup. You learn how to and should handle love through breakups. You can be inspired to look for a better companion or work on yourself to manage love better after a bad relationship. The reasons why getting dumped makes you better include the following.

Your options will be more evident to you. You'll take better partner selection more seriously. Following a breakup, you will be able to clearly identify what you truly desire and what to anticipate from a potential companion. You will be stronger and more confident because you will be more definite and speak up for what you believe is best for your life.

You'll become more self-aware. You'll act with more caution going forward. In the upcoming partnership, you will be aware of what to do and what to avoid. You'll also put in the necessary effort to better yourself, which makes you better.

You are aware that you have experienced a difficult relationship. Therefore, if your new relationship falls apart once more, you will be prepared to handle the stress and heartache. Particularly if your prior relationship was your first love, you will be extremely distraught after the split and feel lonely, empty, hopeless, etc. Nevertheless, you will be a better person in the new relationship if you can recover properly and move on with another one.

You can use other responsibilities to divert your attention from a past failed relationship, such as working more than before, attending counseling sessions, or becoming more devout. These assist you become stronger and more self-assured. Perhaps you'll receive better employment offers, share your experiences to support those who need relationship advice, or

develop your spirituality, all of which
will help you keep a healthy mental and
emotional balance.

CHAPTER 7
AFTER A BREAKUP

Losing your lover through a breakup might be unpleasant for you if there are still times when you find it difficult to forget about them. This is especially true if you previously loved the person very much. You should think carefully about how to handle the breakup and how make yourself better, find a new partner, or assist others.

Get some distance from your ex. Inform them politely that you prefer they leave you alone because you have already ended this relationship. You should refrain from returning your ex's calls, texts, or emails. This aids in mind-clearing so that you can move on with your existing partner.

Plan some activities for you and your buddies. This is an excellent strategy to keep yourself occupied and to temporarily ward off unpleasant emotions. Spend time with your personal buddies. More time should be spent with your current partner. If it's difficult for you not to think of your ex at such time, stay away from your ex and any pals you have in common. Alter your surroundings. Relax at home by listening to mellow jazz, classical, or other music. These have a relaxing impact on you, which also makes you more sentimental, allowing you to express your emotions, cry over them, and then stop thinking about them afterwards. Traveling or moving to a new location, on the other hand, can aid in your recovery.

Avoid overreacting to this breakup. Don't act foolishly just because you are momentarily irritated. Avoid taking actions that could injure you or your partner right now.

Look for ways to get over your heartbreak. Write or paint about what's on your mind. Examine articles. It could be beneficial to read articles published by individuals who share your experiences. Get inspired by reading books. To assist others, you can write about your heartbreaks and publish it online.

CONCLUSION

When you've had breakups in the past and want to stay with your present partner for as long as possible, it's extremely crucial to learn to let go and forgive past mistakes in order to preserve a long-term, healthy, and good relationship. Here are some tips for letting go of the past, whether it involves your ex or your present spouse.

Remain optimistic. Just let it go when you start to feel anxious or unhappy again. Consider the positive aspects of the prior partnership. Remember that your past breakup gave you experience, and you can draw many conclusions from it. Approach situations with positivity. Be honest when breaking up. If you find it difficult to handle it yourself, speak out instead of isolating yourself. Don't keep your grief to yourself and don't hide your emotions. Avoid spending all of your time alone in your room. Additionally, in order to heal more quickly, you must retain an open mind and move on.

Recognize that you are powerless. Even if you're attempting to make things work out after a breakup, you have to realize that you have no influence over your ex or the circumstances.

Talk positively to your loved ones and friends, particularly your partner. Stay away from discussing your past pain and your ex's. Discuss other topics or the problems you are now having while looking for solutions.

Think about the future. Keep in mind that life is short. Take a forward-looking posture. Forgive your ex and the past relationship, and move on. Be aware that the personal roles in your ex's life have ended, even if you two are still friends. Instead, concentrate on your position and duties in the life of your present partner. In addition, do forget and forgive your current partner's shortcomings.